Are you grateful to gobble up turkey on Thanksgiving?

At their first feast, the Pilgrims had many reasons to be thankful.

They had left England and crossed the ocean safely.

They had built a new home in America.

Here, the Pilgrims could pray in their own way.

Here, some of them would own farms for the first time.

But life was not easy for the Pilgrims. They had to do most things themselves.

Pilgrim men built their own houses.

They grew their own wheat and corn for bread.

They hunted
ducks and other
wild animals
for food.

They practiced
being soldiers so
they could protect
their families.

Pilgrim women took care of their homes and children.

They grew vegetables in their gardens.

They cooked food over open fires in their houses.

They baked bread in outdoor ovens.

Pilgrim children did not go to school.

Instead, they learned how to do the work they would do as grown-ups.

But they still
had time to play.

They liked to
blow bubbles
and play
marbles.

The Pilgrims got help from their Indian neighbors.

The Pilgrims traded with the Indians. They gave the Indians tools and cloth. They got animal furs in return.

The Indians showed the Pilgrims the best places to fish.

They also taught them how to grow corn.

The Pilgrims worked hard

and their settlement grew.

The Pilgrims lived a very long time ago.

Their houses and clothes didn't look like the ones we have today.

But the Pilgrims talked and laughed with their friends.

Pilgrim parents loved their children. They tried to make a good life for their families.

The Pilgrims were real people, just like us.